When This Box Is Full

When This Box Is Full

By
Patricia Lillie

Pictures by
Donald Crews

SCHOLASTIC INC.
New York Toronto London Auckland Sydney

The black-and-white photographs were reproduced from line conversions screened with a "Lasergrain" pattern. Color was added by hand with film overlays. The text type is Helvetica Black Italic.

Text copyright © 1993 by Patricia Lillie. Illustrations copyright © 1993 by Donald Crews. All rights reserved. Published by Scholastic Inc., 555 Broadway, New York, NY 10012, by arrangement with Greenwillow Books, a division of William Morrow and Company, Inc. Printed in the U.S.A. ISBN 0-590-48762-0

12 13 14 15 16 17 18 19 09 05 04 03 02 01

Boxes on pages 2-3 and 30-31 from Donald Crews' private collection.

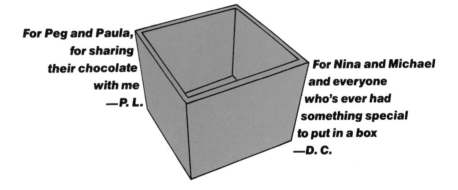

For Peg and Paula,
for sharing
their chocolate
with me
—P. L.

For Nina and Michael
and everyone
who's ever had
something special
to put in a box
—D. C.

This box is empty... but not for long.

I will fill it with...

January

a snowman's
scarf,

January
February
March

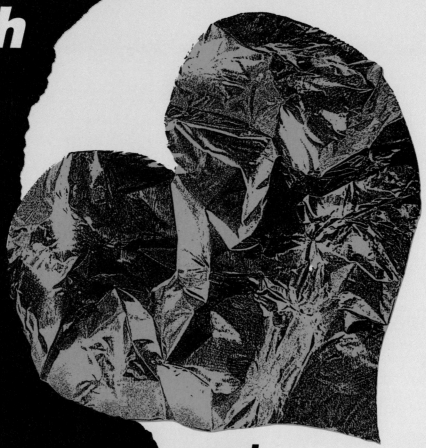

a red

foil heart,

a robin's feather,

January
February
March
April

**a purple
eggshell,**

**January
February
March
April
May
June**

a wild
daisy,

**helicopters
from the
maple tree,**

January
February
March
April
May
June
July

a seashell
and some
sand,

January

February

March

April

May

June

July

August

a ribbon
from
the fair,

January
February
March
April
May
June
July
August
September

a red leaf,

January

February

March

April

May

June

July

August

September

October

toasted
pumpkin
seeds,

January
February
March
April
May
June
July
August
September
October
November
December

a wishbone,

and
a silver
star.

And then...

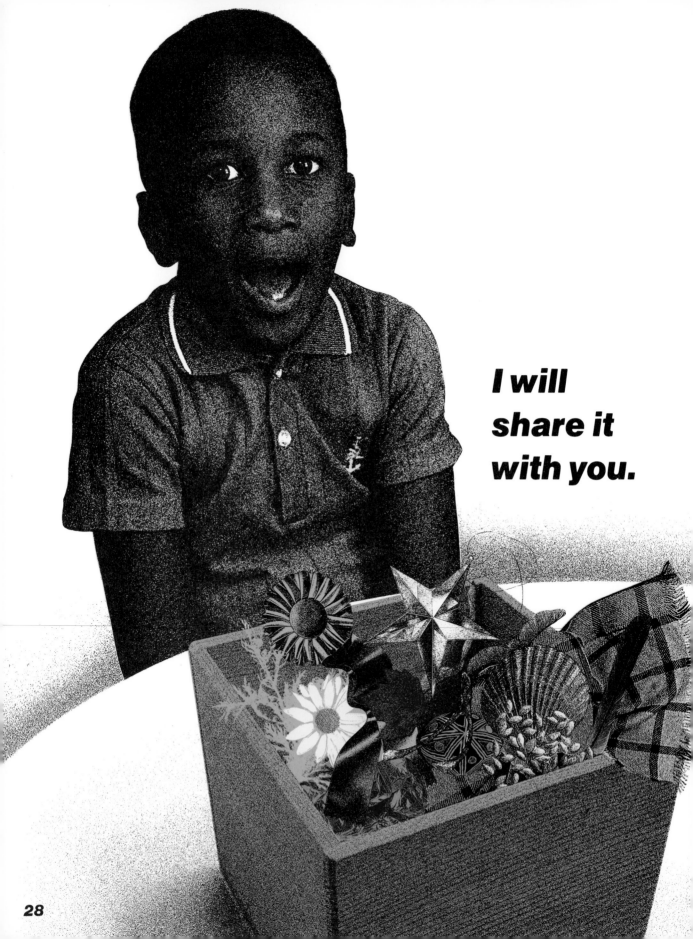

I will
share it
with you.